ANIMALS IN THE WILD

GIANT PANDA

Annette Whipple

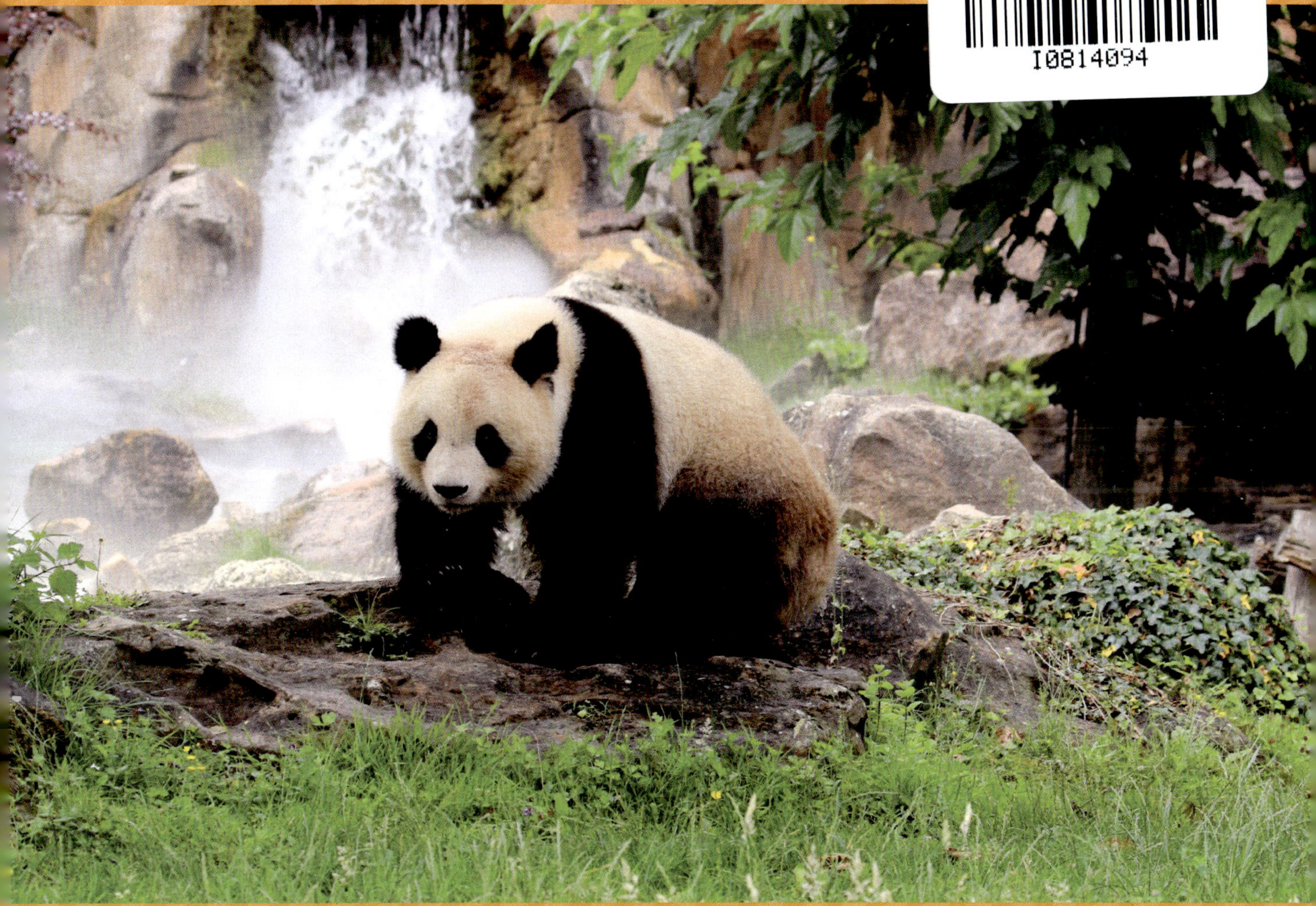

A Crabtree Forest Book

Crabtree Publishing
crabtreebooks.com

Notes for Readers and Class Discussion

This book is designed to teach readers about core subject areas, build curiosity, and inspire further investigation. Readers are encouraged to build upon what they already know about the subject and engage in topics they want to learn more about. Here are a few guiding questions to prompt reflection and discussion. Possible answers appear in red.

Before Reading:

Read the title and look at the table of contents. What do you already know about giant pandas?

- *I know that giant pandas eat a lot of bamboo.*
- *I know that giant pandas only live in the wild in China.*

What would you like to learn about giant pandas?

- *I would like to learn about how big a giant panda is when it's fully grown.*
- *I would like to learn whether the giant panda is endangered.*

During Reading:

Pause after reading each page or chapter. What questions do you have about what you read? What are you curious to know?

- *I wonder why some scientists believed that giant pandas belonged to the same family as raccoons.*
- *I am curious to know why the giant panda is the national animal of China.*

Make connections to what you are reading. How is this like something you already know?

- *I know that some animals are picky eaters that mainly eat one type of food, such as the koala that eats mainly eucalyptus leaves.*
- *I know that one of the biggest threats to animals in the wild is habitat loss due to human actions, such as deforestation.*

After Reading:

Recall key details about the book. What was the author trying to teach readers?

- *The author was trying to teach readers about the characteristics, behaviors, and habitats of giant pandas.*
- *The author was trying to teach readers that giant pandas are a vulnerable species and at risk of becoming extinct if they are not protected.*

How did the images and captions help you understand more?

- *The photographs helped to show me how a giant panda lives and eats in the wild.*
- *The captions helped me understand new details about giant pandas.*

Table of Contents

Meet the Giant Panda

What's black and white and loved all over the world? The giant panda! This cute, fuzzy creature is a national treasure in China—the only country where the animal occurs in the wild.

Pandas are considered endemic to China. This means they are only found in one geographic location.

The "Bear Cat"

The giant panda's name in Chinese means "large bear cat." Their round faces and chunky bear bodies made people think they look like giant cats with bear bodies. Giant pandas are part of the Ursidae, or bear, family. But they also have some non-bearlike behaviors and habits that make them unique.

Mammals

Giant pandas are mammals. All mammals share some of the same characteristics. They keep a constant body temperature even as their environment gets warmer or colder. Hair or fur covers their skin. Females give birth to live young and feed their young with milk the mother produces.

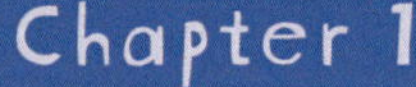

What Do They Look Like?

For decades, biologists debated whether giant pandas were bears. They looked like bears, with a similar body shape and a coat of fur. To end the speculation and find out for sure, scientists researched panda **DNA**. That research took years.

Science Solves It!

In the 1990s, giant panda DNA research revealed that pandas and bears were indeed closely related. The research confirmed that they share common **ancestors**. Giant pandas also look, walk, and climb like bears. They are now considered a "true bear" and part of the Ursidae family.

Some scientists thought giant pandas might belong to the same family as raccoons.

For years, biologists questioned whether giant pandas were bears partly because of their plant diet of bamboo, a tree-like grass.

Black and White All Over

Although they are bears, there are many ways in which giant pandas are unique. Unlike most bears, they are not carnivores, or meat eaters. Giant pandas are mainly herbivores, or plant eaters. They eat mainly one thing: bamboo.

It would be difficult to mistake giant pandas for other bears. Their distinctive white faces and bodies together with their black eyes, ears, shoulders, and legs make them instantly recognizable. Giant pandas grow from around 4 ounces (113 g) at birth to more than 200 pounds (91 kg) as adults.

Panda Size

When giant pandas stand on all four legs, their shoulders can reach 3 feet (1 m) in height. Males weigh as much as a refrigerator—about 250 pounds (113 kg). Females typically weigh a little less. Giant pandas are similar in size to American black bears.

Panda Fur

Like many other mammals, giant pandas are covered with fur. Black patches surround the eyes and cover their ears. Their noses are black. The legs and shoulders of giant pandas are also black. The rest of the body is white. Scientists think the bold black-and-white coloring provides **camouflage** for giant pandas when they're in patches of sunshine in shady forests.

Pelage

The hairy coat, or fur, of a mammal such as a giant panda is called a pelage. The pelage is an **evolutionary** adaptation. This means it has changed slowly over millions of years to best suit the animal's natural environment and ensure survival. The giant panda's unique black-and-white pelage helps it to blend in with both snow and shadows. Its pelage also helps communicate information such as age, health, and sex.

Giant pandas have coarse guard hairs that help repel, or force away, water. Their underfur is woolly and adapted to a climate that is cool and damp.

Other animals that measure 3 feet (1 m) in height include the South American tapir, some Irish Wolfhound dogs, and baby African elephants.

Is That a Thumb?

Giant pandas have six digits on their front paws. These paws look like they have a thumb—but it's not a thumb. Instead, padded skin covers the wrist bone. Biologists call this a "pseudo-thumb." This pad is an evolutionary adaptation that gives the giant panda more precision in handling things, especially food. The pseudo-thumb allows giant pandas to grip and crush bamboo into pieces they can easily eat.

Giant pandas usually grip bamboo in their mouths and hold the stems in their paws using their wrist bones that act as thumbs.

A giant panda's tail is slightly longer than other bear species. Scent glands on the underside of the tail allow the bear to smear its scent.

Strong Skull

Giant pandas have round heads with short muzzles, stocky bodies, and short tails. These features, combined with their black-and-white coloring, make many people think of giant pandas as cute animals. But make no mistake, their skulls and jaws have a powerful bite force—similar to that of a lion.

Teeth for Tearing

The giant panda's teeth are different from other bears. Giant pandas' molars and premolars are wide and flat instead of pointed and sharp. The wide, flat teeth grind and chew the bamboo they eat. Short, blunt canine teeth are made for tearing bamboo.

Chapter 2

Home and Habitat

Giant pandas live on the slopes of China's tree-covered mountains. The temperate, or moderate, climate creates damp forests with dense understories of bamboo. This bamboo provides giant pandas with the food they need.

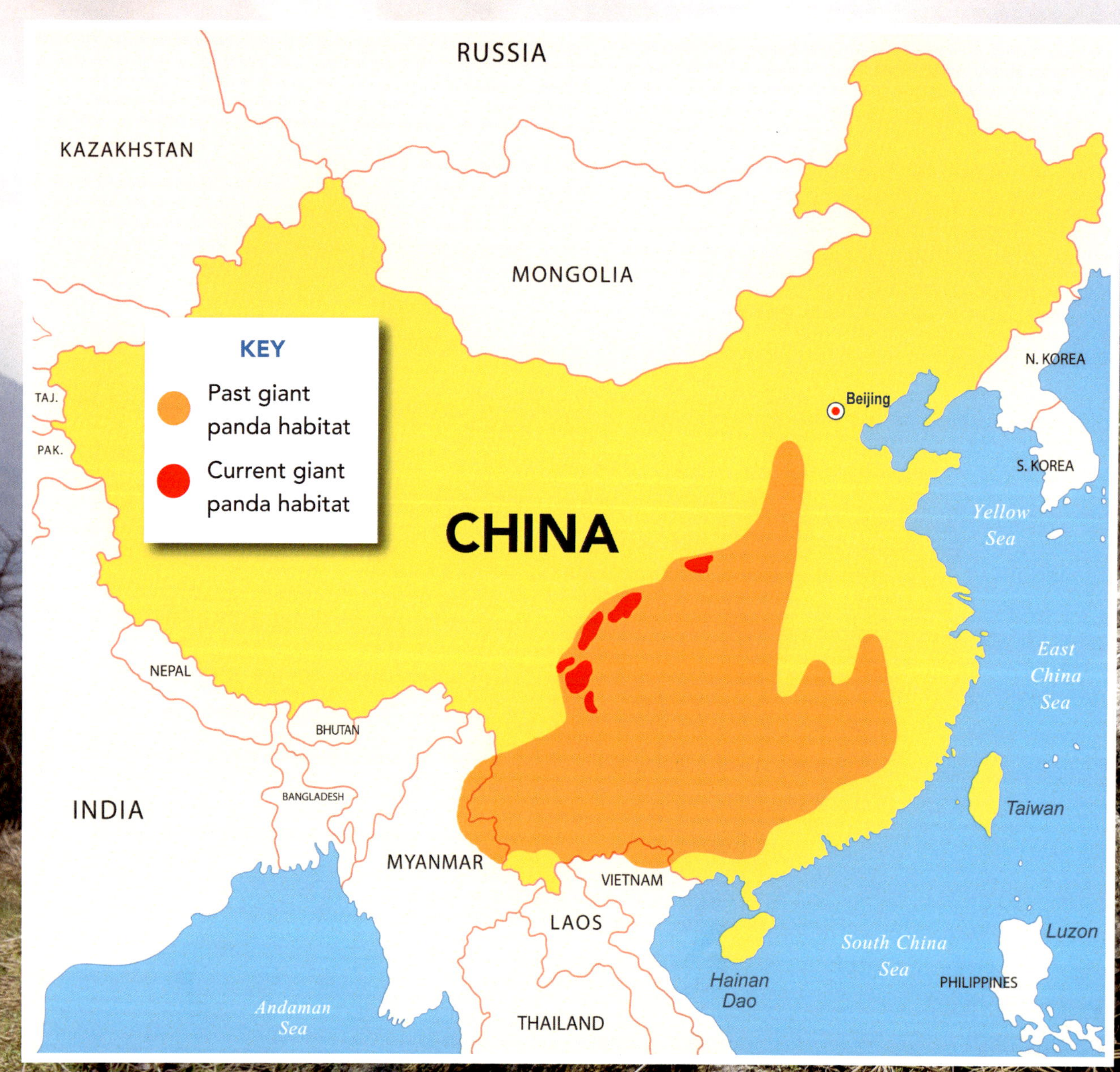

Forest Dwellers

Giant pandas live in environments where their bamboo food source grows. They eat 30 to 60 pounds (14 to 27 kg) of bamboo daily to survive. But pandas need more than just bamboo in their **habitat**. The old-growth forests are thick with trees for shelter, as well as water sources.

Pandas need at least two different kinds of bamboo in their habitat to avoid starving.

Ancient Animals

Fossil evidence shows giant pandas lived millions of years ago in eastern and southern China. Over time, they made their homes at the lower **elevations** of mountain forests. The giant panda's habitat changed over time. This was due to human **encroachment** on their territory and the loss of forest lands.

Most of China's wild giant pandas now live in the bamboo forests of the Minshan mountains of Sichuan province.

Shrinking Habitat

Today, giant pandas live in fragmented, or separate, pockets of remaining forests in Sichuan, Shaanxi, and Gansu provinces. Sichuan is located in China's southwest. Shaanxi is in northwestern China and Gansu is in north-central China.

Active Bears

Unlike other bears, giant pandas do not hibernate during cold winter months. Instead, they move to lower elevations where the temperatures are milder. Their home ranges can cover 3 to 7 square miles (8 to 18 sq. km). **Deforestation** and the rapid development of land by humans have changed the giant panda's habitat over a relatively short period of time.

Giant pandas also used to live in the forests of northern Myanmar and Vietnam. Logging, road, building, and farming forced them out of these habitats.

Industry and Hunting

Industries such as mining, energy production, and intensive farming pushed giant pandas out of their traditional habitat in the 1960s. They were also hunted for food during this time. But efforts have been made to preserve the isolated patches of forest where giant pandas still live. Recently, China's government has been fighting against **desertification** in Gansu province.

Giant pandas prefer to avoid people. As farming and human development spread, they moved into higher elevations.

Pandas in the wild now live in 29 fragmented regions of six isolated forests.

Wet Forests

Giant pandas thrive in year-round damp climates and forests of fir, spruce, and bamboo. In their territories 8,500 to 11,500 feet (2,590 to 3,505 m) above sea level, dense mists and heavy rains commonly occur. Their waterproof fur is well adapted to this climate. Giant pandas shelter in trees and caves, and they often use tree stumps and hollow logs to rest.

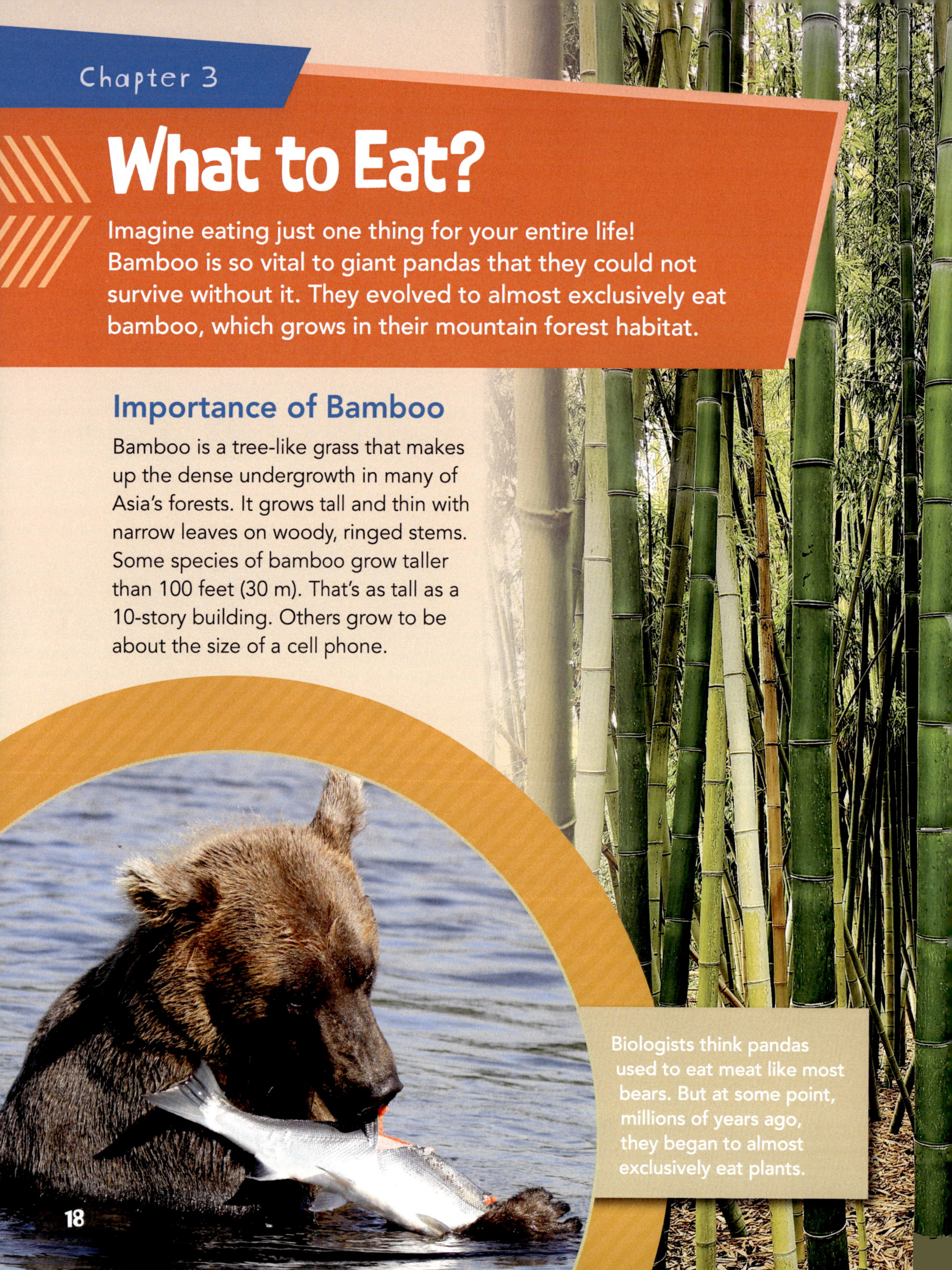

Chapter 3

What to Eat?

Imagine eating just one thing for your entire life! Bamboo is so vital to giant pandas that they could not survive without it. They evolved to almost exclusively eat bamboo, which grows in their mountain forest habitat.

Importance of Bamboo

Bamboo is a tree-like grass that makes up the dense undergrowth in many of Asia's forests. It grows tall and thin with narrow leaves on woody, ringed stems. Some species of bamboo grow taller than 100 feet (30 m). That's as tall as a 10-story building. Others grow to be about the size of a cell phone.

Biologists think pandas used to eat meat like most bears. But at some point, millions of years ago, they began to almost exclusively eat plants.

Pandas basically eat, sleep, and play all day.

Chomp and Chew

How does a giant panda eat bamboo? A giant panda sits upright and pulls a bamboo stalk toward its body. It peels the outer layer of the woody stalk with its teeth. It chews the thick stalks with its strong jaws and flat teeth. The giant panda also strips leaves with its thumb-like pad of skin.

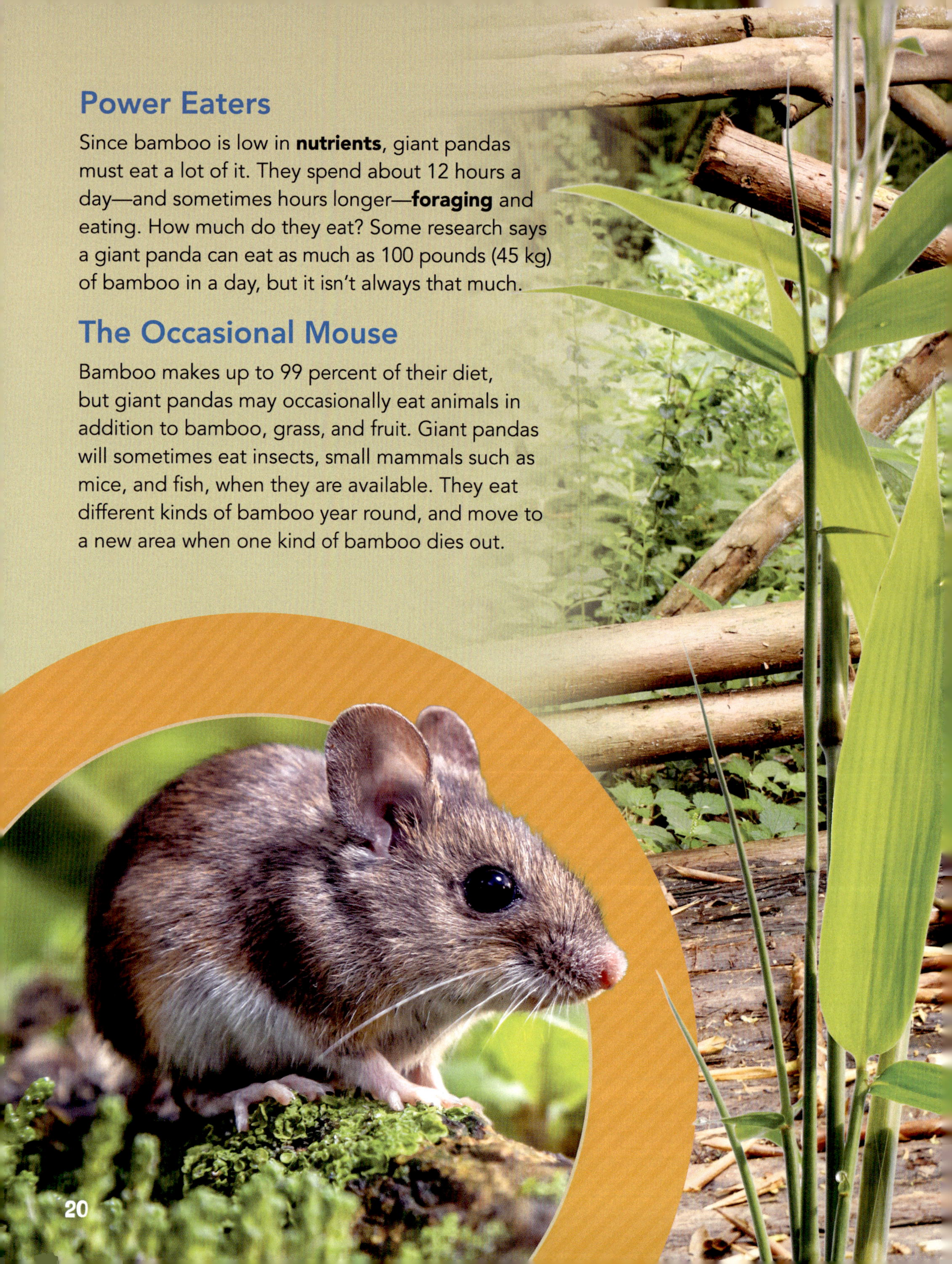

Power Eaters

Since bamboo is low in **nutrients**, giant pandas must eat a lot of it. They spend about 12 hours a day—and sometimes hours longer—**foraging** and eating. How much do they eat? Some research says a giant panda can eat as much as 100 pounds (45 kg) of bamboo in a day, but it isn't always that much.

The Occasional Mouse

Bamboo makes up to 99 percent of their diet, but giant pandas may occasionally eat animals in addition to bamboo, grass, and fruit. Giant pandas will sometimes eat insects, small mammals such as mice, and fish, when they are available. They eat different kinds of bamboo year round, and move to a new area when one kind of bamboo dies out.

Giant pandas are picky eaters and prefer arrow, black, and water bamboo that provide the nutrients they need.

Digestion

Giant pandas eat mostly bamboo, but they have the digestive system of a carnivore. Scientists have been studying their diets for a long time and discovered that despite their grass diet, pandas eat as much protein as wolves and wild cats. About 50 percent of their diet is protein energy. Some bamboo is high in plant protein. But they must eat a lot of it. Studies have shown bamboo altered how pandas grew, behaved, and reproduced.

With a carnivore's digestive system, pandas poop a lot—around 40 times a day. This is because they cannot fully digest all of that bamboo. Their poop is green, like the bamboo they eat.

Feeding in Captivity

Many giant pandas live in zoos around the world. The majority of them are on loan, or borrowed, from China. About 25 zoos in 20 different countries have giant pandas on loan. These zoos signed contracts with China to care for and potentially **breed** the pandas. Many have had the pandas for years, and several have been successfully bred. At the zoos, captive pandas eat bamboo shoots and leaves, as well as fruits and vegetables such as apples, pears, sweet potatoes, and carrots. Some zoos even feed them special fiber biscuits and sugarcane.

Chapter 4

Giant Panda Behavior

Giant pandas are ancient animals. Their ancestors were believed to have originated around the time of the Pleistocine Epoch, or the Great Ice Age, 2.58 million to 11,700 years ago. Over time, giant pandas evolved in physical appearance and behavior.

Low-Energy

With limited nutrition from their diet, giant pandas are low-energy bears. They move while foraging but do little else but eat. They try to avoid stress and high-energy activities. When threatened, giant pandas climb trees or run away.

In 2024, paleontologists found the fossil of a jaw of a giant panda ancestor in southern Germany. Dated to 11.5 million years ago, the bear was an omnivore that ate both plants and animals. It is considered the oldest ancestor of the giant panda.

Sleepy Bear

Giant pandas spend most of their days eating and sleeping. They're **crepuscular** animals, which means they're most active around dawn and dusk. But giant pandas are active at other times too. Both their days and nights include eating and sleeping. Giant pandas sleep in a variety of positions. They might sleep flat on their back or rolled into a ball, but at other times giant pandas lie on their side or stomach.

Pandas are often shown clowning around in photos and videos. They are seen rolling, which biologists say is due to the fact that they lie around so much their muscles get stiff.

Fun and Ferocious

The rear paws of giant pandas point inward, which means they tend to waddle as they walk. They easily stand on their hind legs. They can swim and climb trees. When they aren't eating or sleeping, pandas are known to be playful. They somersault and roll on the ground. But beware—like all bears, giant pandas can be ferocious when threatened. They are very territorial and use scent to mark trees. This sends a message to pandas that are not part of their territory to stay away.

Room to Roam

Since giant pandas need a lot of bamboo every day, they need their own space to forage. They generally live by themselves, and each panda has its own home range. The ranges of male giant pandas overlap quite a bit, while the ranges of females overlap significantly less. When giant pandas meet, they communicate in a variety of ways. They squeak, moan, and chirp. They also rub against each other. Sometimes they even hug.

Communication

Giant pandas mostly communicate through sounds called vocalizations, as well as **scent marking**. Unwanted meetings may lead to growling. Giant pandas might swat and lunge at one another too.

Giant pandas might also seem goofy and clumsy because they have poor vision and sometimes bump into things.

Chapter 5

The Next Generation

In the wild, panda **mating** season usually lasts from March through May. They have a short period of time to reproduce. This partly explains why there are only 1,864 giant pandas in the wild.

Finding a Mate

Although giant pandas are solitary animals who tend to live alone, they know other giant pandas' scents. They reach **sexual maturity** between four and seven years of age. When a female giant panda goes into **heat**, she uses calls and her scent to attract a mate. She only has between two to three days a year during which **fertilization** can occur. She may mate with several males during this time.

Clumsy Mates

Male pandas are not good at the mating game. While female pandas may only be **receptive** to mating for two or three days a year, males often miss the signals females give them. A male giant panda must also stay close to the interested female. Her scent marking signals when she is ready to mate, so the male must be aware and watch for changes in her scent marks before approaching the female.

Giant pandas leave scent marks as long-lasting messages to other giant pandas through chemical smells called **pheromones**. They release a waxy substance from the scent gland under their tail. They leave this wax, as well as smells in urine, or pee, on trees, rocks, bamboo, and bushes.

Giant pandas have an excellent sense of smell. They can find a potential mate by determining when a scent mark was placed.

Low Birth Rate

Unfortunately, giant panda birth rates are low. Females mate just once every two to three years. They may have five litters in their lifetime. Female giant pandas give birth to one or two cubs at a time. If twin cubs are born, however, usually just one survives. The mother often abandons one if she is unable to eat enough to feed two nursing cubs.

The average pregnancy for a giant panda lasts 135 days. Most giant panda cubs in the wild are born between August and September.

Baby Pandas

A newborn giant panda cub weighs only about 4 ounces (113 g). This is about as much as a deck of cards. Giant panda cubs are born helpless and blind. Their skin is pink underneath a thin layer of pale fur that covers their bodies. After about two weeks, the pink skin turns black where their black fur will grow.

Young cubs croak, squeak, and squeal. As they grow, pandas make different sounds such as honking, huffing, barking, and growling.

Den Mother

The giant panda mother creates a den for her cub in a cave or at the bottom of a tree. This is where she cares for her new cub for about six months. The mother's body provides warmth for the cub as it nurses. Mother pandas keep the den clean. They don't want a **predator** to find the cub, so they cover up urine and remove feces, or poop, by eating it.

Panda mothers lick their young to groom them. Licking also helps stimulate the cubs to poop.

Full-Time Job

Panda mothers cradle and cuddle their cubs in their paws and hold them to their chest to help them nurse. A cub can nurse up to 14 times a day for 30 minutes at a time. For the first few days of a cub's life the mother doesn't leave the den at all. When she does leave, it is to eat.

Gaining Independence

After several weeks, cubs open their eyes. They don't move on their own until they are about four months old. For the first year, cubs totally rely on their mother. Sometimes, mothers move their offspring to different den sites—they do this by carrying their young in their mouths. This may be done to keep them safe from predators or to move closer to the mother's food source. At about five months, giant panda cubs begin to wean. This means they start drinking less of their mother's milk and start eating bamboo. Giant pandas grow quickly. Cubs stay with their mothers for about two years. In the wild, giant pandas live for about 20 years.

Zoo Mamas

Zoos throughout the world participate in giant panda breeding programs. These programs have existed since the 1980s. Breeding pandas in captivity is very difficult. Unlike in the wild, where female pandas can choose their own mates, pandas in zoos are paired with other available pandas. These are males brought from other zoos. Since female pandas go into heat just once a year, the mating timing has to be exactly right. After all the effort it takes, zoos celebrate when pandas give birth.

The money zoos pay in loan **leases** is used for **conservation** programs in China. Any cubs born in zoos must be returned to China within four years.

Chapter 6

Giant Panda Conservation

Giant pandas have few natural predators. Their greatest threat is humans and human activities such as hunting and habitat change and destruction. China has been working on giant panda conservation for many decades.

Pandas in China

The giant panda is China's national animal. These bears have been a symbol of the country for thousands of years. In the seventh century, Chinese Empress Wu Zetian wanted to create a stronger relationship with Japan. She gave two giant pandas and 70 pieces of panda fur, or pelts, to the Japanese emperor. The practice of giving or lending giant pandas to strengthen ties and increase goodwill continued throughout the centuries. Eventually, this practice became a conservation program.

In 1972, U.S. First Lady Pat Nixon visited the National Zoo in Washington, D.C., when China gave two giant pandas to the U.S. China now supplies pandas to zoos on 10-year leases of $1 million or more.

Panda Diplomacy

Pandas are symbols of peace, friendship—and political **diplomacy**. Since the 1940s, the Chinese government has given, loaned, and leased pandas to foreign zoos and governments. These pandas were **strategic** gifts and loans. They helped China establish relationships between governments and strengthened trade. Fees are charged by China for the pandas that are on loan. Some of the pandas in foreign zoos were bred, but the lease terms mean the cubs are eventually returned to China. This has increased the numbers of pandas.

Panda Reserves

There are more than 50 reserves for giant pandas in China. These are areas of wild land where pandas are protected from **poaching** and encroachment. About 67 percent of wild pandas live on reserve land. Land reserves are often too small though to accommodate the giant pandas' needs. So sometimes small strips of land are used to connect two or more natural habitats that are separated by human activities or development. These **natural corridors** allow animals to move to different habitats that would otherwise be isolated from one another. Natural corridors keep giant panda populations near one another during mating season while also providing more shelter and food. More corridors would connect even more giant pandas with the resources they need.

Protecting the habitat of giant pandas also helps protect other animals, such as golden monkeys and crested ibises, that live in the same areas.

Vulnerable Species

Currently, scientists consider giant pandas a **vulnerable** species. This means the giant panda species faces risk of **extinction** in the wild based on the threats they face for survival. In the past, giant pandas were named an **endangered** species. Conservation work has increased panda populations in the wild. But while giant pandas are out of immediate danger, they are still not thriving.

Although poaching isn't as big of a concern as in the past, giant pandas are still occasionally hunted for their fur. In some countries, giant panda pelts are still greatly valued by wealthy collectors.

Ecosystem Change

The forest **ecosystem** where giant pandas live is incredibly diverse, or made up of many different species of animals and plants. Giant pandas help their habitat's diversity without even trying. Plant seeds stick to their fur. As giant pandas move, swim, and climb throughout their habitat, the seeds fall off the fur. Then the plants grow and spread throughout the forest.

These animals have lost much of their habitat to deforestation. People cut down forests for logging and firewood. They also clear forests to make room for farming so domestic animals, such as cattle, have a place to graze.

Scientists evaluate a lot of information to decide if an animal species needs help to survive. They look at the total population and if the population is growing, decreasing, or stable.

Surviving While Vulnerable

Giant pandas lose more than their homes when their forest habitat is gone. They lose their primary food source as well as their nesting sites. Cubs are left unsheltered. Survival rates decrease as cubs are exposed to weather and even disease. Without a den's protection, they're also vulnerable to predators such as snow leopards. When habitats are isolated from one another, giant pandas may not be able to find mates during their short breeding seasons.

New road and building construction also contribute to deforestation.

Homes for All

More than a billion people live in China. Just as each person needs a home, so do pandas. Despite conservation efforts, the giant panda's biggest survival issue is loss of habitat. With deforestation, giant pandas have limited access to potential mates, shelter, and food.

Bamboo, the giant panda's main food source, includes many species. Unlike many plants, all members of a single bamboo species die at the same time. This leaves giant pandas searching for new kinds of bamboo. Since forests are often isolated from one another, the movement of giant pandas is limited. This makes it difficult for them to find the food they need to survive.

Rapid city growth is one of the primary causes of deforestation in China, leading to loss of habitat for giant pandas.

Conservation Groups

Conservation groups play a big part in saving wild animals such as giant pandas from extinction. They raise money to preserve habitats and conduct research. They also pressure governments to pass and enforce protection laws. These groups believe the future of all life on Earth is interconnected and that preserving habitats, stopping poachers, and saving one species helps all species—including humans.

The World Wildlife Fund (WWF) was formed in 1961 as a charity to protect wildlife from extinction. The WWF's early work was so connected with giant pandas that its well-known logo depicts the animal.

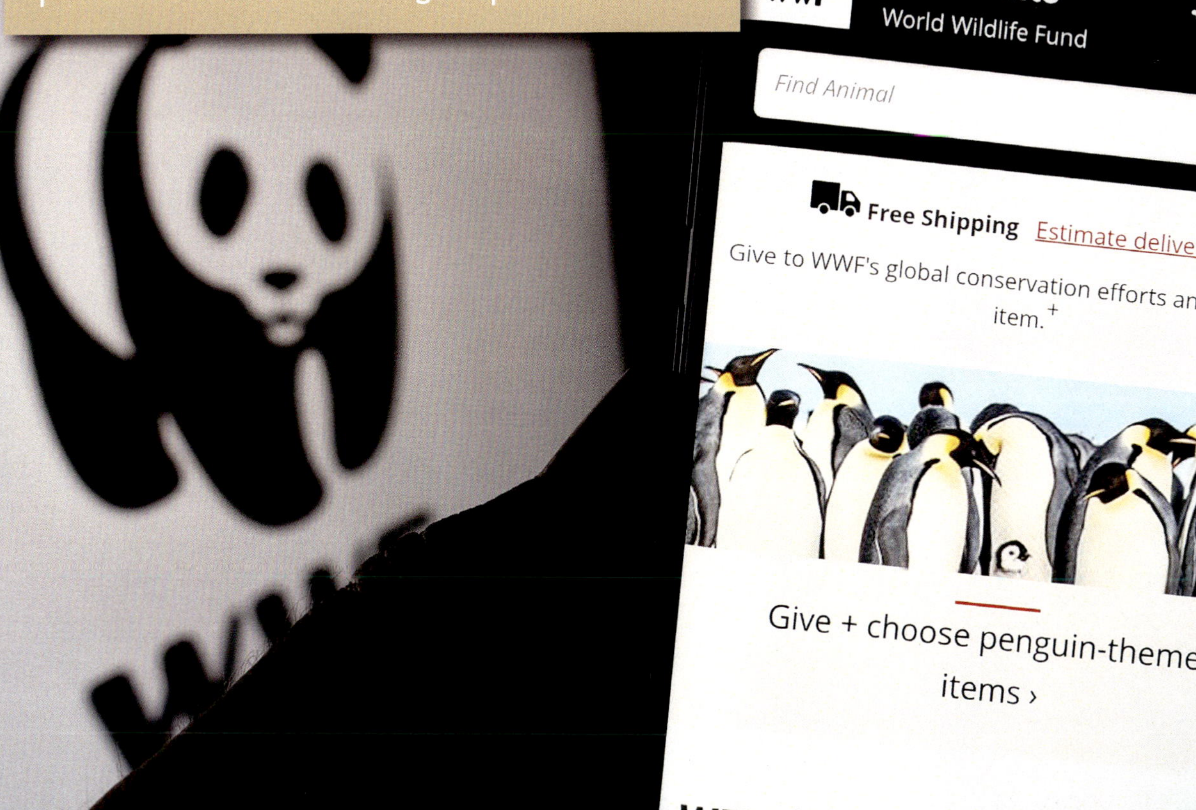

ancestors (AN-ses-ters): Animals in the past from which modern animals developed

breed (breed): To produce offspring

camouflage (KAM-uh-flahzh): Colors and patterns that help an animal blend in with its natural surroundings

conservation (kon-ser-VEY-shuhn): The protection of animals, plants, and their habitats

deforestation (dee-fawr-uh-STEY-shuhn): The permanent clearing of forests or large areas of trees

desertification (dih-zur-tuh-fi-KEY-shuhn): The process by which land becomes dry and turns into desert over time

diplomacy (dih-PLOH-muh-see): The practice of building and maintaining good relationships between nations or governments

DNA (dee-en-EY): A material inside the body's cells that carries all the genetic information about how a living thing will look and function

ecosystem (EE-koh-sis-tuhm): A community of living and nonliving things in their environment

elevation (el-uh-VEY-shuhn): The height of a place, usually measured above or below sea level

encroachment (en-KROHCH-muhnt): The gradual movement of something into an area that is beyond the usual limits

endangered (en-DEYN-jerd): An animal or plant species that is considered to be at a very high risk of becoming extinct in the wild

evolutionary (ev-uh-LOO-shuh-ner-ee): Relating to the process in which animals and plants change over a long period of time to survive better in their environment

extinction (ik-STINGK-shuhn): When an animal or plant species completely dies out and disappears from Earth forever

fertilization (fur-tl-uh-ZEY-shuhn): A key step in reproduction, when an egg and sperm join

forage (FAWR-ij): To search for food

habitat (HAB-i-tat): The place where an animal or plant naturally lives and grows

heat (heet): When a female animal is in a state where she is ready to mate

lease (lees): A legal agreement that allows someone to have something for a period of time in return for payment

mating (MEY-ting): When a male and female animal join together for the purpose of producing offspring

natural corridors (NACH-er-uhl KAWR-i-dawrs): Designated areas of land and water that allow animals to move safely between habitats

nutrients (NOO-tree-uhnts): Substances in food that animals, people, and plants need to live and grow

pheromone (FER-uh-mohn): A chemical substance that an animal produces to communicate with other animals of the same species

poach (pohch): To catch or kill an animal illegally

predator (PRED-uh-ter): An animal that hunts other animals for food

receptive (ri-SEP-tiv): Capable of or willing to receive

scent marking (sent MAHR-king): A behavior by some animals in which they use scents produced by their bodies to communicate with other animals

sexual maturity (SEK-shoo-uhl muh-CHOOR-i-tee): The stage when an animal becomes capable of reproduction

strategic (struh-TEE-jik): Relating to a detailed plan meant to achieve a particular goal

vulnerable (VUHL-ner-uh-buhl): An animal or plant species considered to be at high risk of extinction in the wild

INDEX

COMPREHENSION QUESTIONS

1. The giant panda is the national animal of __________.

a. Australia
b. Thailand
c. China

2. True or False: Giant pandas hibernate during the winter.

3. True or False: Giant pandas are most active around dawn and dusk.

4. In the wild, giant pandas live for about ____ years.

a. 7
b. 12
c. 20

5. True or False: Giant pandas have few natural predators.

6. Giant pandas are similar in size to ______.

a. American black bears
b. polar bears
c. grizzly bears

7. The giant panda's name in Chinese means ______.

a. black-and-white raccoon bear
b. large bear cat
c. bamboo bear

8. True or False: Female giant pandas give birth to four to five cubs at a time.

ANSWERS
1. c, 2. False, 3. True, 4. c, 5. True,
6. a, 7. b, 8. False

About the Author

Annette Whipple is the author of many children's books, including *The Laura Ingalls Wilder Companion: A Chapter-by-Chapter Guide, Whooo Knew? The Truth About Owls, and Quirky Critter Devotions: 52 Wild Wonders for Kids.* When Annette's not reading or writing, you might find her baking for her family in Pennsylvania. Get to know her at AnnetteWhipple.com.

Written by: Annette Whipple

Editor: Ellen Rodger

Proofreader: Melissa Boyce

Design and layout: Tammy McGarr

Production manager:
Candice Campbell

Image Credits

Shutterstock: Matyas Rehakp 35 (right), HARITH SAQEEF p 36, TonyV3112 p 42 (bottom), T. Schneider p 43 (top), John M. Chase p 43 (bottom)

Wikimedia Commons: Creative Commons p 22 (bottom), public domain p 37 (top left)

All other images from Shutterstock

Crabtree Publishing

crabtreebooks.com 800-387-7650

Hardcover 978-1-0398-7480-0
Paperback 978-1-0398-8434-2
Ebook (pdf) 978-1-0398-8193-8
Epub 978-1-0398-8313-0

Published in Canada
Crabtree Publishing
616 Welland Avenue
St. Catharines, Ontario
L2M 5V6

Published in the United States
Crabtree Publishing
347 Fifth Avenue
Suite 1402-145
New York, New York, 10016

Library and Archives Canada Cataloguing in Publication
Available at Library and Archives Canada

Library of Congress Cataloging-in-Publication Data
Available at the Library of Congress

Printed in the U.S.A./CP022026